I0813777

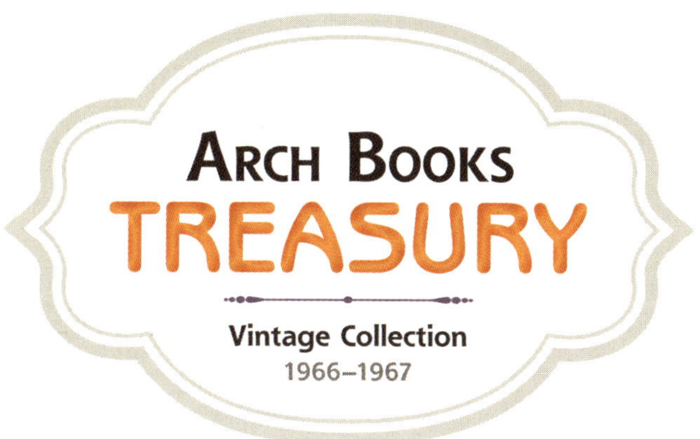

12 CLASSIC ARCH BOOKS

CONCORDIA PUBLISHING HOUSE · SAINT LOUIS

Arch® Books

Published 2016 by Concordia Publishing House

3558 S. Jefferson Ave., St. Louis, MO 63118-3968

1-800-325-3040 • **cph.org**

Manufactured in Noida, India/061664/417186

3 4 5 6 7 8 9 10 11 12 32 31 30 29 28 27 26 25 24 23

Table of Contents

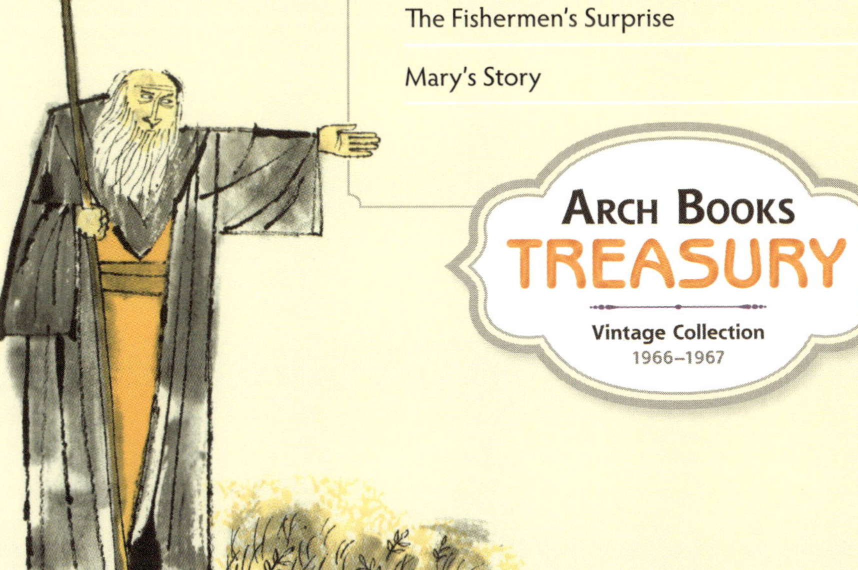

Arch Books
TREASURY

Vintage Collection
1966–1967

Dear Parents,

Let the children come to Me, and do not hinder them, for to such belongs the kingdom of God.

Luke 18:16

Parents and educators are given the wonderful responsibility of teaching children about God and His will for them. One of the ways we do this is by teaching them God's Word—the Bible. From its beginning in the mid-1960s to today, Arch Books have existed for the sole purpose of teaching the Bible to children. More than 400 different Arch Books have been published so far. And through them, millions of children have learned about biblical people and events, about faith and forgiveness, and about the Gospel of Jesus Christ.

Now, as this beloved series enters its sixth decade, Concordia Publishing House is rereleasing these Arch Books to commemorate its legacy and to celebrate its influence on Bible literacy. This collection is a reproduction of original words and pictures.

To God be the glory!

The editor

QUALITY RELIGIOUS BOOKS FOR CHILDREN
ARCH BOOKS
the Great Escape
How God Set His People Free

the Great Escape

the Great Escape

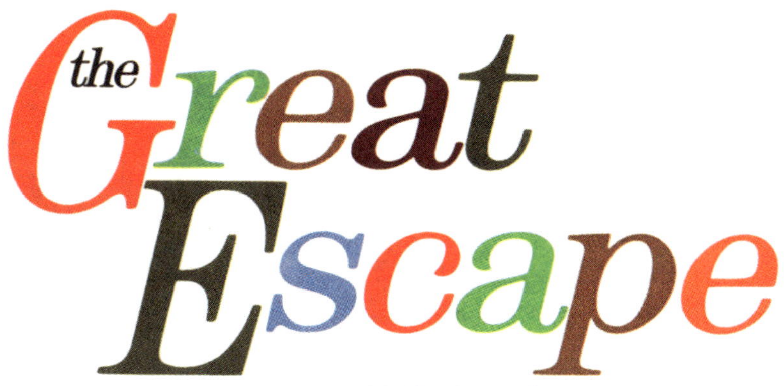

EXODUS 3:1–15:1 FOR CHILDREN

Written by Mary Warren
Illustrated by Jim Roberts

Concordia Publishing House

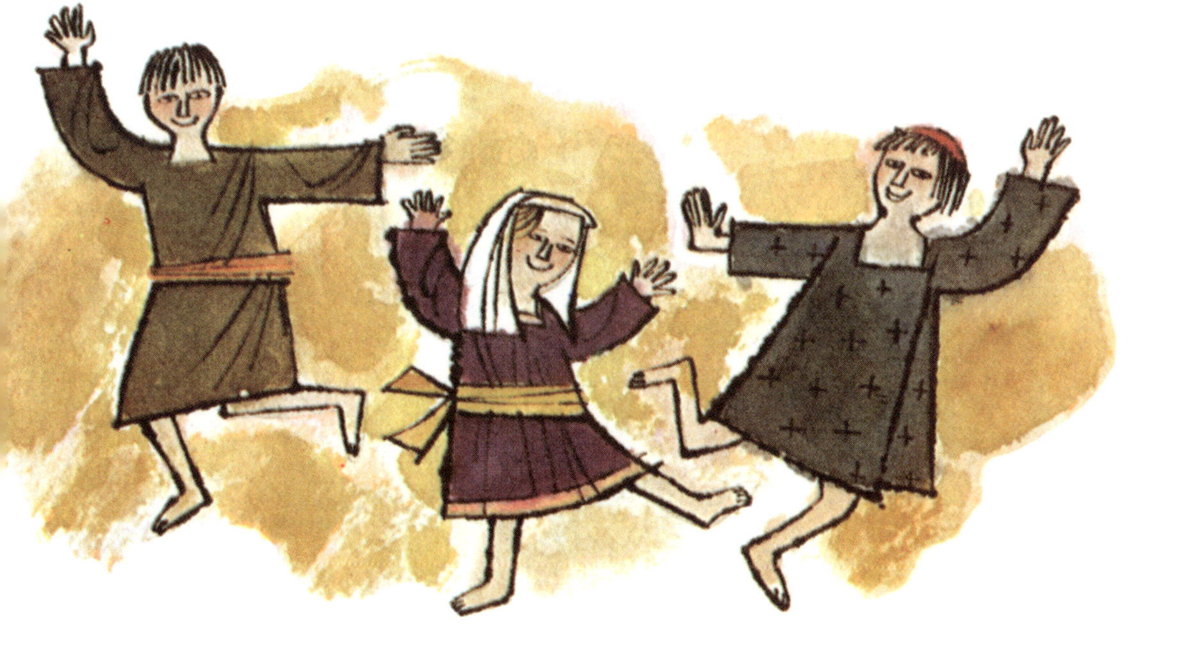

"Passover time is here again!"
the skipping children sing.
"Unleavened bread with roasted lamb
to our table bring!"

The youngest children ask: "But why is dinner strange tonight?"
Their father says, "It tells us of the story of our flight.

“Long ago when Moses
was grazing his flock one day,
he saw a bush burst into flame
and heard a strange voice say:
‘I am the God of Abraham,
Isaac . . . and Jacob too.
The promise I once gave to them
I surely will bring true.

" 'The sadness of My children down in Egypt saddens Me. I'll show you how to help Me make My people free.'

"Moses went to Egypt
and there, in blistering sun,
he watched his people making brick.
Their work was never done!

“He found his brother Aaron
and told him of God’s plan:
‘Please go to Pharaoh with me;
you are a bolder man!’

“Inside the mighty palace,
before the golden throne,
they bowed down low to Pharaoh
and made God’s wishes known.

"Pharaoh listened to them,
dismissed them with a nod:
'Why should I free the Hebrews?
I do not know your God!'

"He felt so cross he made his slaves
work twice as hard and long.
'I am the ruler here,'
he cried.
'That Hebrew God is wrong!'

“God sent plagues to Pharaoh’s land:
all water turned blood-red.
A million frogs hopped all around.
At last the Pharaoh said:
‘Tell your God to end these plagues!
I’ll let your people go.’ But when
the ugly frogs had disappeared . . .
he changed his mind again.

"God sent flies and other bugs
and families got sick;
but after every plague, the king
soon tried his same old trick.

"He made all sorts of promises.
The Hebrew people heard!
But when things started to go well,
he broke his promised word.

"At last God had enough.
He said to Moses, 'Listen!
Tonight when darkness fills the skies
and stars begin to glisten,
I will send my Angel, Death,
to take Egyptian sons.
If Hebrew doors are marked, he'll know
your homes are not the ones.'

“Then God told Moses what to do:
They all prepared a feast.
They killed their first-born lambs, and used
some blood from every beast
to mark their doorways as a sign
for Death to pass them by.
They mixed their dough without the yeast,
though children wondered why!

"Late in the night, Egyptians rose
and wept; Death made them sad.
When Pharaoh's servants wakened him
he cried, 'This news is bad!'

"He summoned Moses, Aaron too,
and muttered: 'Go, I say!
Tell your people they must leave!
Please take them far away!'

"In haste the Hebrews packed their tents,
their bowls with dough for bread;
(there was no time to raise it then;
they'd eat flat bread instead).

"Small children stumbled sleepy-eyed.
Their parents tried to hurry.
'The Pharaoh still might change his mind!'
This was the constant worry.

"They started for the Promised Land,
the Lord knew every need:
His flame would light the way each night.
By day, His cloud would lead.

"They camped nearby the sea named Red.
At night somebody shouted: 'See!
The Pharaoh's chariots have come!
Oh hurry, we must flee!'

"God's cloud made all the sky pitch black.
It filled the way between
the Hebrews and the army, so
no people could be seen!

"God made a wind push back the waves;
it left a bridge of sand.
The Hebrews hurried over it,
their freedom close at hand!

"Pharaoh's army quick gave chase,
but — with a roaring sound —
the walls of water covered them
and many men were drowned.

"With beating hearts, the Hebrews sang a prayer of victory.
They praised the Lord for saving them.
They shouted: 'We are free!' "

Dear Parents:

The exciting story of the exodus from Egypt belongs to Jews and Christians alike. Had God not brought the Hebrews out of their slavery, the entire history of mankind would have been different.

The Lord freed the Hebrews from their oppression both because He is grieved by the suffering of His people and because He was faithful to the promises He had given to the "fathers," Abraham, Isaac, and Jacob. He had a special plan for the Hebrew people. Through their history God's saving will and love was to become known to mankind. In Jesus Christ, a son of the Jewish people, Abraham's family became a blessing to all the earth.

The first Christians, familiar with the Passover from their childhood on, saw in the deliverance from the bondage of Egypt and the Passover lamb a foreshadowing of Christ's victorious and redeeming sacrifice, delivering us from the slavery of sin and the doom of death. Christ is the "Lamb of God" to Christians, and His Supper the new Passover meal, in which we taste the freedom He has won for us. This is why churches even use unleavened bread on the occasion.

Will you help your child understand our story and see the greatness of God's concern and love for His people in this story of deliverance? And can you help him fit it into God's promises and plan with His people?

THE EDITOR

QUALITY RELIGIOUS BOOKS FOR CHILDREN
ARCH BOOKS
THE BOY WHO SAVED HIS FAMILY
THE STORY OF JOSEPH AND HIS BROTHERS

THE BOY WHO SAVED HIS FAMILY

GENESIS 37–50 FOR CHILDREN

Written by Alyce Bergey
Illustrated by Betty Wind

Concordia Publishing House

Once there was a boy named Joseph.
He was one of thirteen children.
Their father was Jacob.
Their family had lived in the land of Canaan
ever since their great-grandfather Abraham.

Jacob owned many animals.
His children took care of the sheep and goats.

Jacob loved Joseph best of all his sons.
He gave him a long coat with long sleeves;
this showed that Joseph was to be the leader.
The boy was very proud of his coat.

His brothers could see that their father
loved Joseph more than any of them.
They hated Joseph because of this.

Once Joseph told his brothers:
"I dreamed we were tying
bundles of wheat.
Your bundles bowed down to mine."
This made the brothers angry.

Another time Joseph told them, "I dreamed that the sun and moon and eleven stars bowed down to me." "Do you think we will bow down to you?" the brothers laughed.

One day Joseph was looking for his brothers.
"Let's kill the dreamer," they said
when they saw him coming.
"No," said the oldest brother.
"Let's put him in this deep hole."

So they took away his new coat and put him in the deep hole.

Just then some men rode by.
"Would you like to buy a boy?"
the brothers called out.
"You could sell him in Egypt."
"Yes, we will buy him," said the men.

The brothers put goat blood
on Joseph's coat.
When Jacob saw the coat, he cried,
"A wild beast has killed my boy."
He was very sad.

On his way to
Egypt Joseph cried,
"Will I ever see Father again?
Why did my brothers do this to me?"

Then Joseph thought:
"God can make bad things turn out good." Joseph wasn't so afraid anymore.

In Egypt Joseph was sold to a rich man. He had to work without pay. But his master liked his work, and God was with him.

One night the king of Egypt
sent for all his wise men.
He said: "I dreamed that I saw
seven fat cows and seven thin cows.
The thin cows ate up the fat ones.

"Then I saw seven good ears of wheat
and seven bad ears of wheat.
The bad ears ate up the good ones.
What does this mean?"
But none of the wise men knew.

Then one of his servants said,
"Joseph knows the meaning of dreams."
The king sent for him at once.
Joseph was a grown man now.

Joseph explained the dreams:
"O king, for seven years
much food will grow,
and for seven years nothing will.
Store up food in the good years.
Then there will be food
for the bad years."

"You are very wise," the king told Joseph. "Take care of things for me."

The king gave Joseph
new clothes,
and the king's ring
and carriage.

Soon the seven good years came.
Everything grew so that Joseph
had to have new barns built
to store the wheat.

Then came the bad years.
But people could buy food
from Joseph.

So Joseph's big brothers came, too.
They bowed way down before him.
They did not know he was Joseph.
But he knew them.

"You are spies!" he said.
"Oh, no, sir!" they cried.
"We have come only to buy food
for our family."

"No, you are spies," Joseph said. "Put them in jail!" he ordered.

After three days the brothers were taken back to Joseph. "Now we are paying for what we did to Joseph," they whispered, afraid.

Joseph heard
what they said.
He felt sorry
for them.

“I am Joseph, your brother!” he cried.
“I am not angry with you anymore.
God brought me to Egypt
to save us all from hunger.”

The brothers were so happy! They had long been sorry for what they had done to Joseph.

They went to get the whole family.

How happy Jacob was!
"Lord," he cried, "You are taking such good care of us."

God said: "I shall go with you to Egypt. Someday I will bring your family back and give them this land."

Jacob and his children moved to Egypt.
Joseph cried for joy when he saw his father.

The family got sacks of flour,
and good grass land for their animals.
And God was with them.
But one day they would return home.

Dear Parents:

The story of Joseph is not just an adventure tale, standing all by itself. It is a story about how God can change even the worst things into something good and wonderful in His own good time. It forms a part of the great adventure of the people of God, Israel, and of God's saving plan for mankind.

God had brought Joseph's great-grandfather Abraham into the land of Canaan, there to bring up a new people who would differ from all the surrounding nations by their faith in Him. Nothing could block God's saving plan; not even such disasters as famine or the actions of Abraham's great-grandchildren could. Sold into slavery by his brothers, Joseph became God's instrument in the saving of Egypt and his own people from hunger. The family tragedy became their salvation, and eventually ours because it was from Abraham's family that the Savior of all nations was to be born.

Can you help your child see the deeper meaning of the Joseph story and recall it in times of fear and anxiety? And will you help him grow not only in knowing the various Bible stories but also in understanding how they belong to one great plan of God?

THE EDITOR

QUALITY RELIGIOUS BOOKS FOR CHILDREN
ARCH BOOKS
DANIEL IN THE LIONS' DEN

DANIEL IN THE LIONS' DEN

Written by Jane R. Latourette

DANIEL 6 FOR CHILDREN

Illustrated by Sally Mathews

Concordia Publishing House

Have you heard of Daniel,
a brave Jewish man
whom the king of Ba-by-lon
put into a lions' den?
Why was he punished so?
And what happened then?

Prince Daniel served the King,
who liked him so
it made the other princes mad.
"Let's get rid of him," they said.
"But isn't it too bad
we cannot say old Daniel does
a single thing that's wrong?
We'll have to trick him
some sly way.
We'll watch him all day long."

Now, other men in Ba-by-lon
prayed to a lot of different gods.
But Daniel,
all the long years through,
to our own God was always true.

These jealous men
saw Daniel go
into his room next day.
They listened on the ground below,
as Daniel knelt to pray.

"Aha!" they cried.
"This helps our plan!"
And to the palace these men ran.

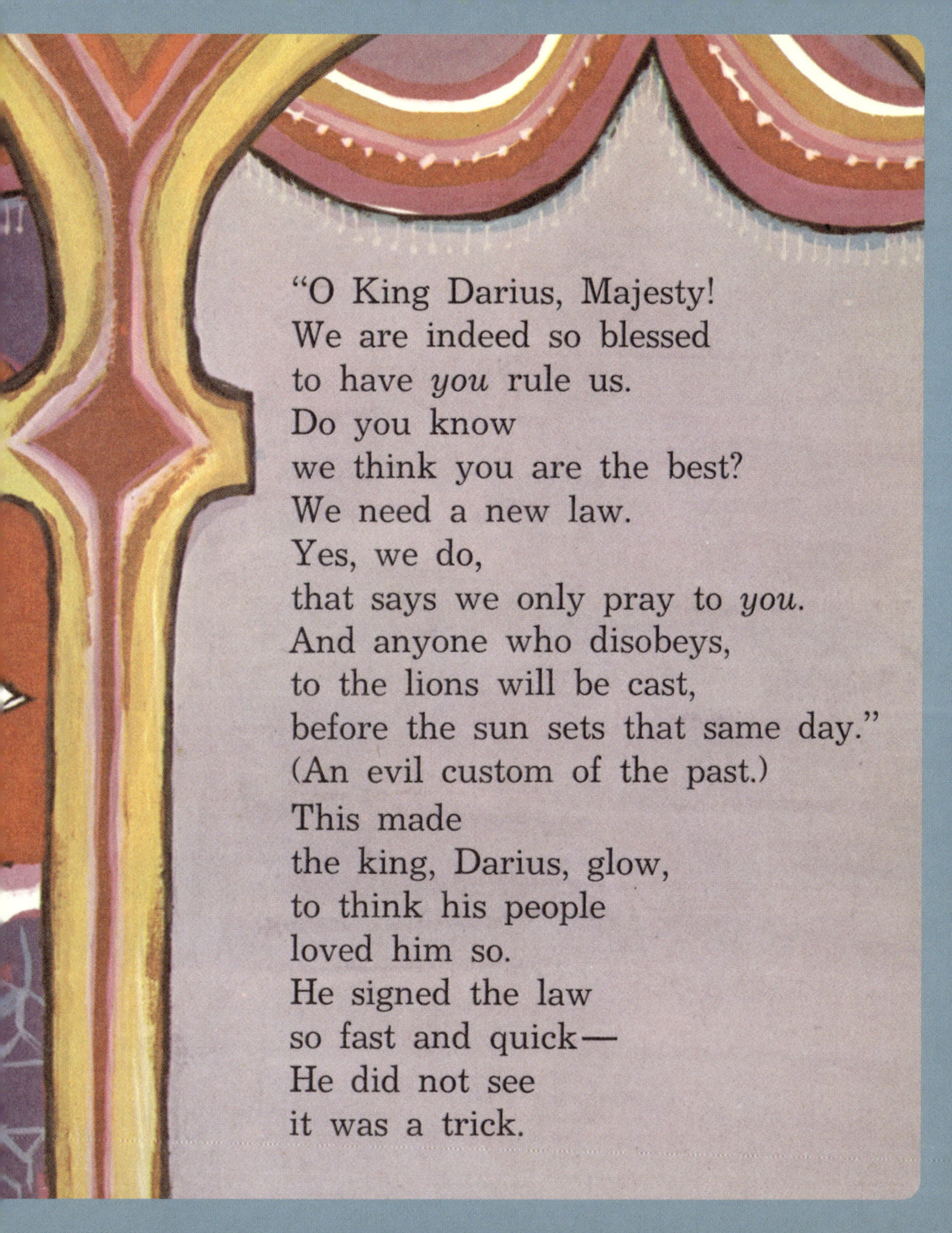

"O King Darius, Majesty!
We are indeed so blessed
to have *you* rule us.
Do you know
we think you are the best?
We need a new law.
Yes, we do,
that says we only pray to *you*.
And anyone who disobeys,
to the lions will be cast,
before the sun sets that same day."
(An evil custom of the past.)
This made
the king, Darius, glow,
to think his people
loved him so.
He signed the law
so fast and quick—
He did not see
it was a trick.

But Daniel was a brave old man.
He heard the news
(and saw the plan).
Yet *still* he stopped three times a day
to give thanks to our God, and pray.

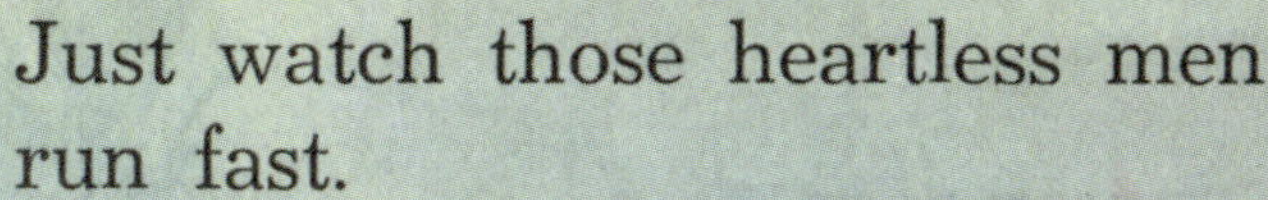

Just watch those heartless men
run fast.
"Your Majesty! We just went past
old Daniel's room.
We heard him pray
to his own God, the same old way.
He is the *first* to disobey!"

The king cried out, "Not Daniel!
He's done no wrong. You know it."
"But," these men shout,
"A law is law.
It *must* be kept.
Now show it!"

No help for Daniel.
He's marched then
at sundown to the lions' den.

They push him in.
The lions roar.
The guards clang shut
the heavy door.

The king's in tears,
he's so upset.
He spends the night awake.
"Dear Daniel.
Oh, if he should die,
I think my heart will break."

At dawn, the king then hurries
to the lions' den.
So worried, he can hardly breathe,
he shouts, "Oh, Daniel,
tell me, please.
Could your God save you
from the lions' teeth?"

"Yes," Daniel calls.
"My God shut tight
the lions' mouths
all through the night.
Please don't be sad.
I'm quite all right!"

The king is overcome
with joy.
He makes the guards
let Daniel free.
(The wicked men
are soon destroyed—
thrown in the pit
of snarling beasts.)

To all his people,
far and near,
the king sends out this word:
"Now hear!
Let us praise the God
who has saved Daniel
from the power of the lions.
He works many wonders.
He saves and He rescues.
The God of Daniel is the King
over heaven and earth!"

My, what a celebration then
was held to honor Daniel—
This man who'd faced the lions' den,
so *sure* God could take care of him!

Dear Parents:

The story of Daniel is a story about the "God who works wonders." Which was greater: the amazing rescue of Daniel from the power of the lions or the rescue of Daniel from the fear of both beasts and men?

It was difficult to stay loyal to God and to act upon one's convictions when most people around believed and acted differently. To stay true to God and disobey the law of the land was to face a sure and gruesome death. "But Daniel to his God stayed true," convinced that God was able to save him even out of a lions' den. And, if we may add a thought from another part of the Book of Daniel, even if God did not save him, he would still stay true to Him (Daniel 3:18). Daniel had deep roots in the faith and prayer life of the Jewish community, with its experience of God's faithfulness throughout its history.

Will you help your child see in this story God's marvelous power not only over beasts but also over the hearts of men? And will you help him be nurtured and sustained by the faith of the Christian community, as Daniel was by his? When we know God's faithful love in Jesus Christ we can face even the "lions' den" in trustful obedience to God.

The Editor

QUALITY RELIGIOUS BOOKS FOR CHILDREN

ARCH BOOKS

THE HOUSE ON THE ROCK

A PARABLE ABOUT GOD'S WORD

THE HOUSE ON THE ROCK

Written by Jane R. Latourette
Illustrated by Sally Mathews

MATTHEW 7:24-27 FOR CHILDREN

Concordia Publishing House

By a river, long ago,
in far-off Galilee,
two men set out to build new homes:
John and Zebedee.

They chance to meet along the road,
their donkeys small beneath their load.
"Greetings, Friend! Where are you bound?"
says John to Zebedee, who frowned—

(I hope I get there first, thinks he—
That sandy place is just for me)....

"Oh, guess I'll look along this side,
right where the river spreads out wide.
I'll find some sand to build upon—
a day or two, I'll have it done!

"And are you going over yon?"
asks Zebedee of his friend John.

"Yes, there's a hill-top spot I've found,
with bright red flowers all around.
From way up high, there's quite a view,
and *solid rock* to fasten to."

Each takes his donkey and supplies
and starts to work 'neath fair blue skies,
with river gurgling in between—
the gentlest stream you've ever seen!

Look! Zeb is done in two days flat.
No foundation—he just skipped that.
He doesn't think what might go wrong;
now hear him sing his care-free song:

“Oh, tweedle-dum and tweedle-dee,
no work, just *fun,* for Zebedee.
Get by as easy as I can,
that’s why I choose to build on sand!
Oh, I’m the man who builds on sand,
builds on sand,
builds on sand,
Oh, I’m the man who builds on sand,
come dance and sing with me!”

For many days, beneath the sun,
John's family works to get theirs done.

Foundation first—and then the blocks,
with songs that ring across the rocks.

To celebrate, when work is done,
they join their neighbors for some fun.

A feast, some songs, some games for all;
but say—those clouds look like a squall!

Lightning zig-zags 'cross the sky;
the angry clouds come roaring by.
Thunder crashes—the rain begins—
great gusts of rain, pushed by the winds.

John's family runs for home, pell-mell;

Zeb's family, frightened, starts to yell.
"What shall we do? What shall we do?
Look, Pa, the river's rising, too!"

They scramble to the second floor,
but still the water rises more,
and slowly swings the house about,
this way—that way—There's no doubt

they need to clutch at some loose log,
and hold on tight, all four—and dog!

John's house shakes some, and slightly sways,

but on that rock it stoutly stays.

He suddenly sees his neighbors' plight,
he rushes down from his safe height,
and pulls Zeb's family on their log
straight in to shore—all four, with dog!

Now, warm and snug, they all look out
upon the flood, and round about.
Of Zeb's new house there's not a trace;
just water now where was his place.

He shakes his head, does Zebedee,
"Why did I act so foolishly
to think a house could stand
if built on nothing more than sand?"

A brilliant sun comes bursting through,
and makes a rainbow—what a view!
The bright red flowers merrily
lift up their lovely heads to see.

And the river settles back
to its old familiar track.

Dear Parents:

Our story is based on a parable Jesus told about His teachings. When a person hears what Jesus has to say and bases his life on it, he will be like a man whose house has a solid foundation. No floods can undermine it; no winds can sweep it off.

But the man who hears what Jesus says but lives as if it had nothing to do with him builds on a shallow and flimsy foundation. His life is headed for a disastrous surprise.

Can you help your child understand the point of the story? And will you help him build his life on solid rock, not by threats, but by the way you guide him and shape the life of your family?

THE EDITOR

QUALITY RELIGIOUS BOOKS FOR CHILDREN
ARCH BOOKS
THE LAME MAN WHO WALKED AGAIN

THE LAME MAN WHO WALKED AGAIN

MATTHEW 9:2-8 FOR CHILDREN

Written by Mary Warren
Illustrated by Betty Wind

Concordia Publishing House

When Jesus taught in Galilee,
a lot of people came
because they heard that He could heal
the deaf, the blind, the lame,

the folks who could not talk at all,
and some on stretcher beds,
and those with fits and stomachaches,
and others with hurt heads.

Some mothers carried babies small
too sick to make a cry.
And Jesus healed the lepers too,
and any passing by
who had a fever, crippled arm,
or any kind of pain.
And people who were feeling sad
He soon made laugh again!

There was one man who could not move.
He wept,
he wanted so
to go to Jesus to be healed.
He watched the others go.

His wife went out to ask his friends
if they might find a way.
"Why sure!" they cried, "We'll carry him.
Come! Let us go today!"

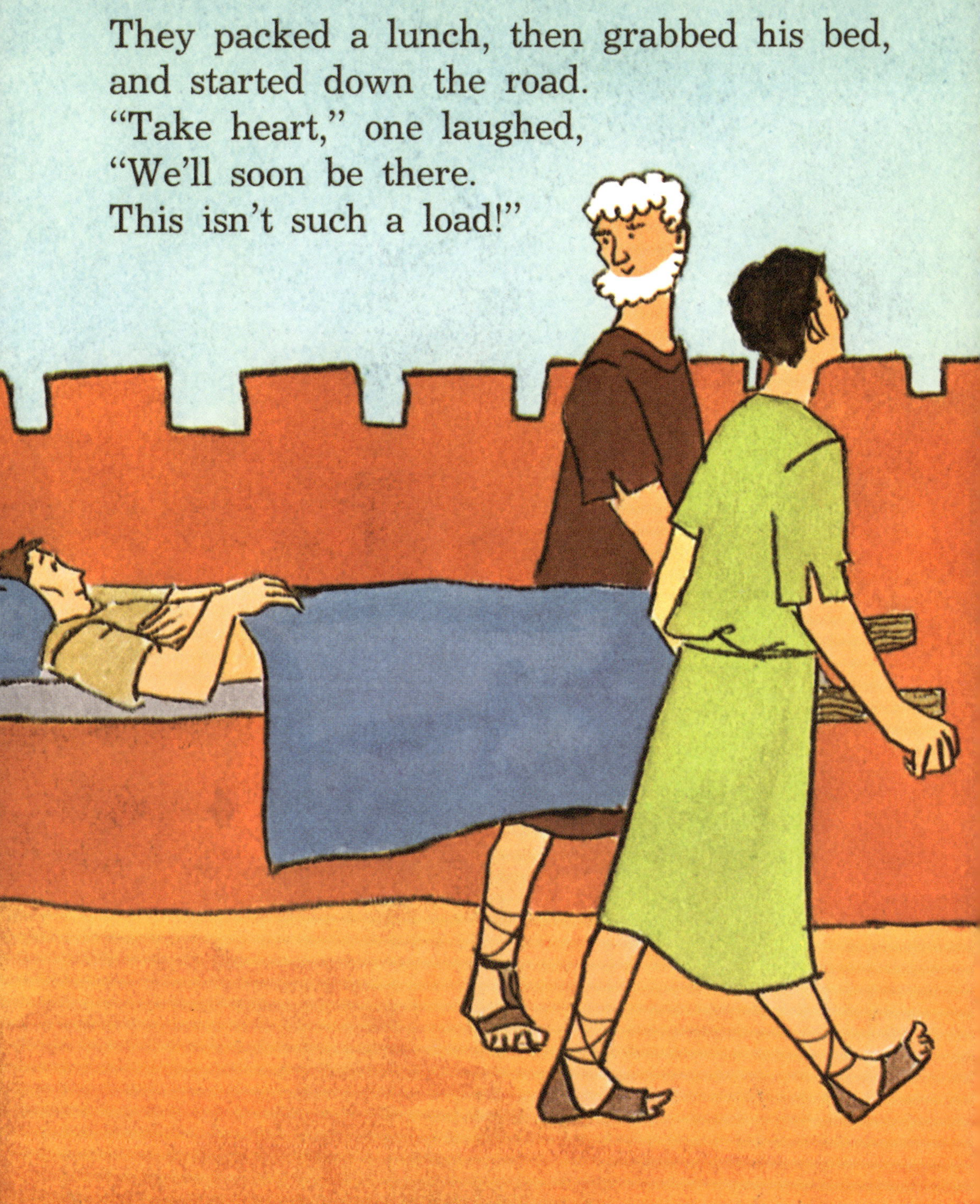

They packed a lunch, then grabbed his bed,
and started down the road.
“Take heart,” one laughed,
“We’ll soon be there.
This isn’t such a load!”

"I think I know the house," one called,
"It isn't hard to tell.
I see a mob of people there . . .
and some already well!"

Sure enough—one man had thrown
his crutch away in glee;
and another shouted out:
"My eyes are healed! I see!"

But when the friends got to the house they could not reach the door. So many people crowded in there was no room for more.

"Don't give up, we'll find a way;
we won't go home," they said.
So, as they walked around the house,
the man watched from his bed.

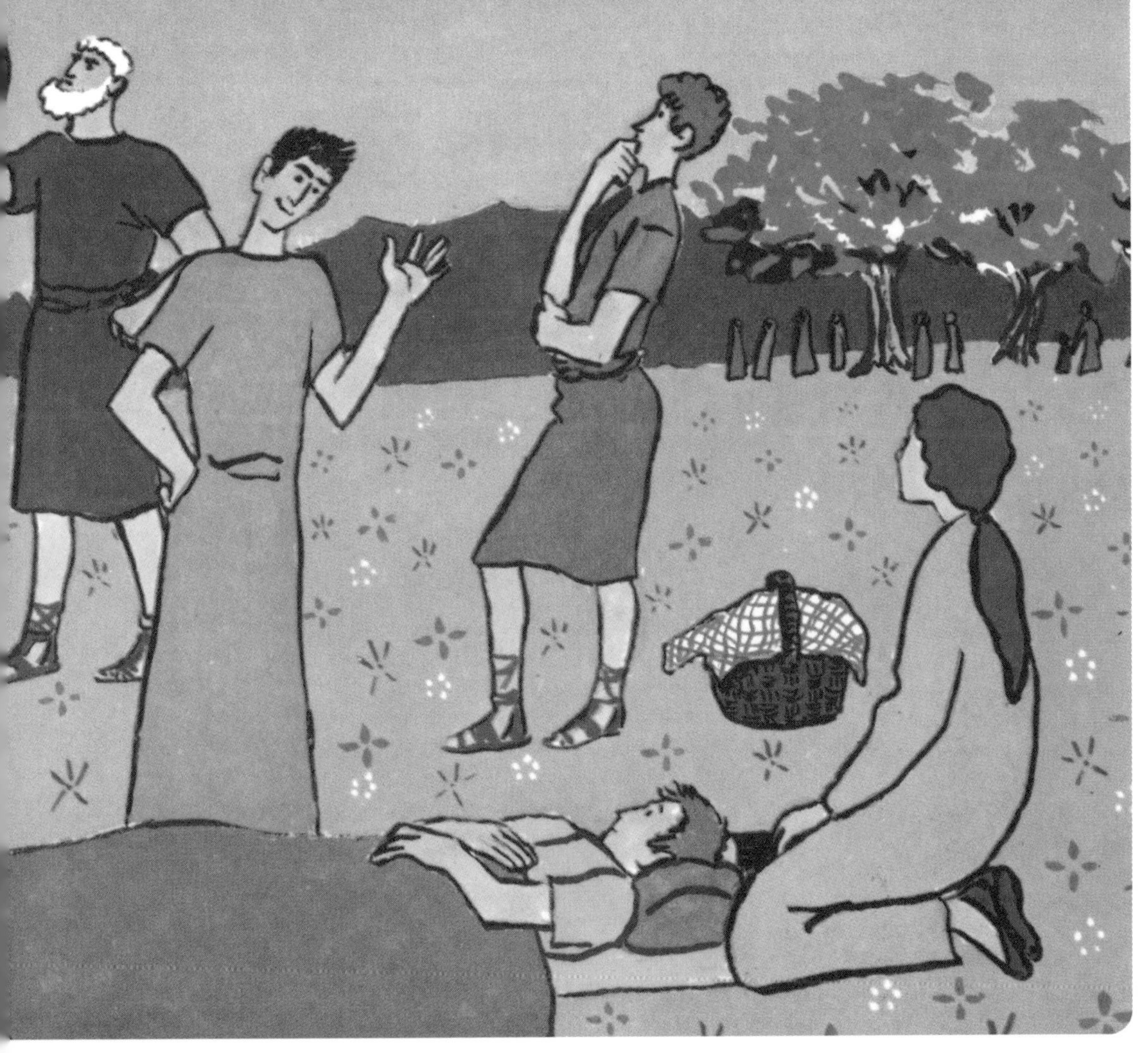

At last one had a clever thought.
"Oho! the roof!" he cried.

“Now hang on tight and up we’ll go!
O! What a bumpy ride!”
To hoist the sick man to the roof
they tugged with all their might.
A few who stood there watching smiled
at this unusual sight.

"These tiles are loose; let's take them off and lower him right down!"

The startled people in the house jumped back: "Who is this clown?"

But Jesus watched how tenderly
the friends set down the bed.
He saw the sad and worried eyes
the sick man had, and said,
with kindness in His voice: "My son,
your sins I take away."
Some people thought: "This cannot be!
Is this for man to say?

"It's only God who can forgive.
That right is only His!
This man is rather arrogant.
Who does He think He is?"

But Jesus said:
"I can forgive!
It's not a bunch of lies.
I'll show you what I mean:
Young man,
fold up your stretcher!
Rise!"

The sick man up
and shouted: "Thanks!"
He danced around in joy.
He hadn't felt so full of life
since he had been a boy!

He tied his stretcher in a roll;
the people watched, amazed.
They raised their hands toward heaven high
and cried out: "God be praised!

"What Jesus says is true! Just look!
This man whom He forgives is well!
Let's hurry back to all our friends . . .
We have good news to tell!"

Dear Parents:

Jesus was concerned about the whole man — not just about his soul or just about his physical well-being. But because the different parts of man hang together, Jesus heals both body and soul.

Our story shows Jesus' love and understanding of each man and his troubles. The Gospel doesn't claim that our lame man was sick because he had committed some sin (otherwise we would all have to be sick all of our lives). But Jesus sensed the burden of guilt the lame man was secretly carrying. That is why Jesus forgave the man before healing him.

The main point of the Gospel here is that Jesus has the authority to forgive on God's behalf. We don't just *hope* that God will forgive. We receive the *certainty* of our forgiveness through the Savior He has sent and those who act in His name. (John 20:21-23)

Can you help your child think of Jesus as someone who can and does forgive us when we have been bad, so that the past is past and we can move about with the carefree heart and confidence which belongs to God's children? And will you help him sense the reality of God's forgiveness by accepting God's forgiveness yourself for your own failures and those of others, especially in your own family?

THE EDITOR

QUALITY RELIGIOUS BOOKS FOR CHILDREN

ARCH BOOKS

THE SECRET OF THE STAR

THE STORY OF THE WISE MEN

MATTHEW 2:1-12 FOR CHILDREN

Written by Dave Hill
Illustrated by Jim Roberts

Concordia Publishing House

ONCE, in a far-off Eastern land,
on a night so long ago,
a wise old man named Melchior
was pacing to and fro.

Now Melchior was a Magi priest,
who knew each star by sight.
"At least I DID," he told himself,
"until this star tonight
burst in the skies to dazzle my eyes,
and make me wonder why
one strange new star outshines by far
all others in the sky."

But he didn't know, and so... "Oh, ho!
Yes! That's the thing to do!
I'll send for Caspar and Balthasar!"
Perhaps... perhaps they knew.
He clapped his hands and gave commands,
sending for them to come.
"With three wise men... perhaps... why not?
Aren't three heads wiser than one?"

From the frost-painted North,
where the winter winds danced,
golden-haired Caspar came riding.

From the sun-blistered South,
where the summer breeze pranced,
came black, bearded Balthasar striding.

"You see that star?" said Melchior,
"Now — why is it so bright?"
"Perhaps it means," young Caspar said,
"that somewhere on this night
some great, great thing has come to pass."

"Of course!"

"That's it!"

"You're right!"

"Yes, yes, of course," they said as one,
"but now — just what great thing?"
"A battle?" "A war?" "A fire?" "A flood?"

"A poet?"

"A prince?"

"A king?"

“A KING! A KING!” they shouted in glee,
“A king is born tonight.
That’s why this star shines from afar,
filling the earth with light!”
“I think . . . I read . . .” said Balthasar,
“in some old musty book . . .
About a star . . . to beckon from far . . .”
“To work!”
“To work!”
“Let’s LOOK!”

They read, and read, and read some more,
until old Melchior spied
an ancient holy Jewish scroll:
"That's it! That's it!" he cried.

"See? — Read! It says a Star will come
from Jacob — which means the Jews.
Their King will rule the world in peace!
This star brought us the news!"

"Quick! Get a map! We'll have to go,
and gifts, too, we must bring.
God sent this star — we'll follow it
and worship this great King!"

"Load up the camels!"
old Melchior cried.
"This trip will take us far!"
The camels were packed,
and they set out,
led on by one bright star.

For days and days, and weeks and weeks,
through heat and wind and sand,
the star led on until at last
they reached the Holy Land.

"Jerusalem!" cried Melchior.
"We're there, beyond a doubt!
The star — it moves no more!"
"So now let's find the newborn King.
Let's go and search Him out.
We'll ask from door to door!"

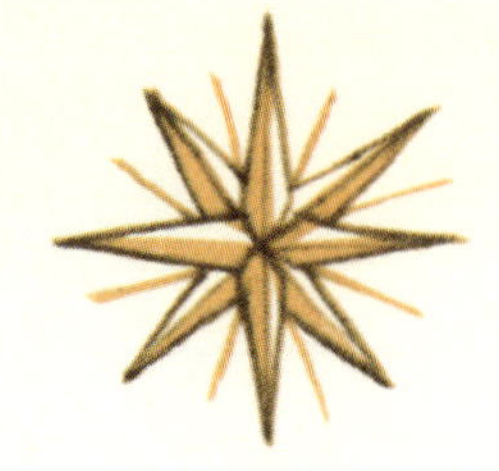

"A King?"
"A Star?"
"No, I've not heard."
"A King's been born, you say?"

"A Prince?"
"Of Peace?"
"Don't be absurd!"
"You're mad — please go away!"

I'LL SHOW THEM

But old king Herod on his throne
soon heard of everything.
He sent his guards to bring them in —

WHO'S THE KING!

For in his heart the mighty king
was full of hate and fear.
"Another King? This can't be true!
I'll have no rivals here!"

H

"I hear you've come to see the king.
Well, look — for here I stand!"

But Melchior just shook his head,
"But, don't you understand?
We seek a Prince of Peace, and Love,
a Savior of the land!"

They left the king and searched some more,
till Bethlehem they found.
"He's here! He's here!"
old Melchior cried.
"The star shines all around!"

They found the house
where Jesus was,
and knew at once that He
was God's own Prince of Peace—
the One they'd come so far to see!

They gave their gifts of frankincense
and myrrh and gold, and then
knelt down in awe to praise the Lord
for His great Gift to men.

"God sent the star," said Melchior,
"to lead us to the Lord.
We'll take the good news back with us!
We'll spread the joyous word!"

Then silently, with singing hearts
and wondrous news to bear,
they journeyed to their own home lands
to tell the people there
about the Prince of Peace God sent
to save men everywhere!

Dear Parents:

The story of the "wisemen," or the "magi," the learned astrologers from the East who were led by a star to the Christ Child, is a story of the Light given to the Gentiles (nations) in Christ the Messiah. The appearing of Christ to the world is what we celebrated on Epiphany, the "Twelfth Day of Christmas."

For about 2,000 years the descendants of Abraham formed a people apart from the rest of the nations. It was in their history that God made His ways and will known, preparing for Himself a people that would bring His revelation to the ends of the earth when the time was ripe. The promise was that at the coming of the Messiah the "nations" should flock to the Light come to Israel (Is. 60:1-6). Those who did not know God's glory should then receive a "sign" and come and see it (Is. 66:18-21). This was now beginning to be fulfilled with the coming of the wisemen, whom ancient Christian tradition sees as three men named Caspar, Balthasar, and Melchior, symbolically representing all the different peoples of the earth.

Will you help your child see the excitement involved in the sign given to these heathen magi inviting them to see and welcome the Christ Child, the Prince of Peace, the Savior and King of all the earth? You may want to act out their journey and celebrate their happy arrival and thus discover a meaningful way to close the Christmas season.

THE EDITOR

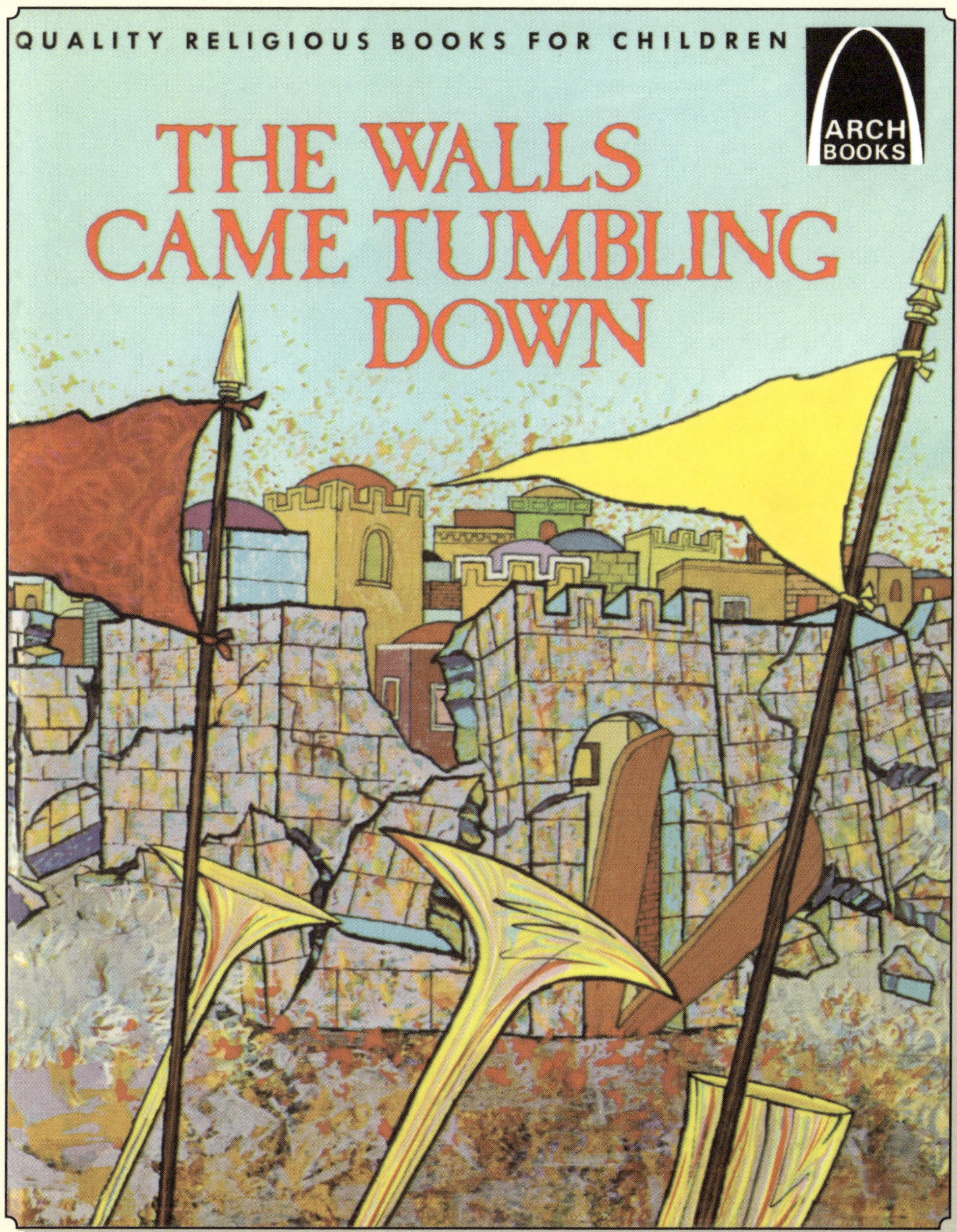
QUALITY RELIGIOUS BOOKS FOR CHILDREN
ARCH BOOKS
THE WALLS CAME TUMBLING DOWN

THE WALLS CAME TUMBLING DOWN

JOSHUA 1–6 FOR CHILDREN

Written by Dave Hill

Illustrated by

Jim Roberts and Art Kirchhoff

Concordia Publishing House

When God had led His people through
the desert long years past,
He told them of the Promised Land
He'd lead them to at last.

Now River Jordan lay ahead,
beyond that – Canaan Land,
their own to take as soon as God
would lead them with His hand.

God chose a man named Joshua
and gave him this command:
"Over Jordan lead My people
to the Promised Land."

But just across the river wide
sat high-walled Jericho.
So Joshua picked out two spies
and said to them: "You go
and see how strong the city is.
Come back and let us know.
For big, strong men live in that town,
and they will stand and fight!
So you two men must go and spy
on Jericho tonight!"

The spies reached Jericho by night
and quickly sneaked inside
the walls to have a look about.
But then a soldier cried:
"Who are you strangers over there?"

And they ran off to hide.

"Come here, you men – I'll help you hide!"
they heard a woman call.
They raced inside her house, which sat
upon the city wall.

"You men must hide," the woman said,
and Rahab was her name.
"Up on the roof – I'll hide you there.
I am so glad you came,
for all the folks here are afraid –
we hear of you, you see.
And I know God is on your side.
He gives you victory."

She covered them with mats of reeds
until the soldiers passed,
then brought them down and said to them:
"You'll have to leave here – fast!"

She set a basket on the floor
and took a rope – bright red –
and tied the basket to it tight.
"Now get inside!" she said.
"I'll let you down the city wall
and leave the rope to show
my house – so when your soldiers come,
they'll let my family go."

The spies ran back to Joshua
and happily cried out:

"The people are afraid of us!
We'll win without a doubt!"

But others shouted, "Where's the bridge?
Just see that water run!"

"God moved with us," said Joshua,
"in all things we have done.
And He will hold the waters back.
We march with morning sun."

At dawn the priests marched with the ark
down to the riverside.
The Ten Commandments, carved on stone,
were safely held inside.

They stopped to pray, then walked right in
and held the ark up high.
"A miracle!" the people cried,
for Jordan had gone dry!

Across the empty riverbed
the people marched all day.
Then Joshua, the general, said:
"Let us all kneel and pray
and thank the Lord for this good land
He gave to us today!"

Next day they marched to Jericho
and camped about the wall.
"It's high!"
"And strong!"
"And thick!"
they said.
"But God will make it fall!"

They marched and marched
around the walls
with seven trumpets playing.
The soldier men of Jericho
up on the wall were saying:
"Such noise they make –
what silly folks!
Why don't they go away?"

But they just blew their horns
and marched
around the wall that day.

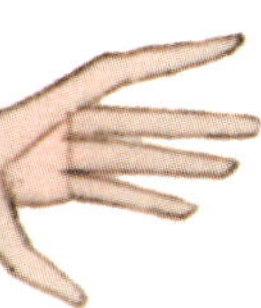

For six long days they did the same;
then came the seventh day.

"Today we win," said Joshua.
"Let's hear your trumpets play!"

With trumpets loud the people marched
around the walls so high
for seven trips – and then they stopped
and raised a mighty cry! ! !

A sound of thunder filled the land
and rumbled all around,

as mighty Jericho's great walls

CAME TUMBLING TO THE GROUND!

Said Joshua: "Go take the town,
but Rahab shall go free,
for now she wants to serve the Lord
with all her family."

“We have a home,”
the people cried.
“God gave us victory.”

Dear Parents:

The story of how the walls of Jericho came tumbling down is part of the great adventure of God's people.

God had called Abraham to leave his home and venture into the unknown. He promised him and his children a new homeland in the land of Canaan. At a later time his descendants became slaves in Egypt. After many years God led the Hebrews out of slavery. Forty years they wandered in the Sinai desert region. Only the next generation had the faith to venture into the land of Canaan, inhabited by "people greater and taller" than they, with "cities great and fortified up to heaven." (Deuteronomy 1:28)

God gave Joshua the faith to lead his people across the Jordan to possess Jericho, the fortress city at the entrance to the Promised Land. Now this homeless people had a home, a land in which they could freely develop into the kind of people God had in mind when He had chosen them to bear a blessing for all the nations of the earth. (Genesis 12:2-3)

Will you lead your child to see how our story fits into the plan of salvation God had for His people? Will you help him see that Joshua marched against Jericho on the strength of God's promise? Will you help your child believe that God has ways to pull down walls in our lives today?

The Editor

QUALITY RELIGIOUS BOOKS FOR CHILDREN
ARCH BOOKS
The Man Caught By A Fish

The Man Caught By A Fish

THE BOOK OF JONAH FOR CHILDREN

Written by M. M. Brem

Illustrated by Jim Roberts

Concordia Publishing House

When God looked down on Nineveh,
that city made Him sad
because the things its people did
were almost always bad.

"The way they live must change," God thought.
"A prophet must be sent."
So God told Jonah he should go
and tell them to repent.

But Jonah didn't want to go:
"I just can't waste my time
on strangers who don't love my Lord
and are not friends of mine.

"I just won't go to Nineveh!"
So Jonah left that day
and bought a ticket on a ship
that went the other way.

He went aboard and looked around
the inside of the ship.
"Since God won't find me here," he thought,
"I'll rest up on my trip."

But as he slept, God sent a storm
with winds that were so strong
that soon the sailors were afraid
their ship would not last long.

And as the waves became so high
that they could sink the boat,
they threw their cargo overboard
to keep their ship afloat.

But nothing helped. Then someone said,
"The storm was sent because
of something one of us had done.
To find him, let's draw straws."

And Jonah drew the shortest straw.
They asked, "Are you the one?
Has your God sent this storm on us
because of what you've done?"

And on the slippery deck he faced
the men. His face was grim.
"I tried to run away from God,
but one can't run from Him.

"I know these winds and mighty waves
were sent here by my Lord.
So if you want to stop this storm,
just throw me overboard!"

"We can't do that," they cried aloud.
They tried to row instead.
It didn't help. So in the end
they did what Jonah said.

As soon as he was overboard,
the sea was calm again,
and all the men knelt down and prayed
to God our Lord right then.

As Jonah sank beneath the waves,
he couldn't hold his breath.
But God had sent a mighty fish
to rescue him from death.

The fish swam up, mouth opened wide,
and swallowed Jonah down.
So in the belly of the fish
God didn't let him drown.

Three days and nights he cried to God
because he was afraid.
"You should have gone to Nineveh,"
God told him as he prayed.

"To you the Ninevites are strange,
but they're My people, too.
You should have brought My Word to them
as you were told to do."

And then God sent the fish toward land,
and with a mighty cough

the fish dumped Jonah on the sand
and turned and then swam off.

And Jonah knew what he must do.
He had a second chance.
He started off toward Nineveh
without a backward glance.

And when he got to Nineveh,
he preached all through the town.
"In forty days you all will die!
My God is coming down.

"You wonder why? Just look around!
You see the things you do.
And most of what you say and think
is mean and wicked, too!"

They hung their heads in shame. Some cried.
They didn't even eat.
They put on rags, took off their shoes,
and walked in their bare feet.

As God looked down, He saw their hearts
had changed. They understood.
And so He thought, "I won't destroy
them as I said I would."

Then Jonah went outside the walls
to watch the Lord come down.
"Those forty days have long since passed.
God should destroy this town!"

Now God had caused a plant to grow
to give him extra shade.
But Jonah only sat and sulked
inside the booth he'd made.

"I'll just stay here," he told himself,
"where I can watch the town."
And as he sat, he was surprised.
The leaves were falling down!

"What is the matter here?" he said.
"Now I have lost my shade."
And in the stem he saw a hole
he thought a worm had made.

He bent and looked. "I think a worm
has killed it," Jonah said.
And he was angry with the worm
because the plant was dead.

But then God came and spoke to him.
"What kind of man are you?
You feel so sorry for a plant–
why not this city, too?

"Just think how happy they must be.
Why do you have that frown?
The angels cheer when ONE is saved;
through you I saved a TOWN!"

Dear Parents:

The story of the "man caught by a fish" is not just a tale about some poor fool who found out you can't run away from God and then was rescued in a fantastic way—by a huge fish. The main interest of the Book of Jonah is the pagan city of Nineveh and how God and an upright believer felt about the people there.

To a righteous Israelite like Jonah the Assyrian capital of Nineveh was just a den of wickedness, a people who did not believe in the true God. They were outsiders who in his view had no claim on the concern and compassion of those who were "in." The Ninevites were strange and morally corrupt. Why bother with them?

Yet God does not share Jonah's feelings of superiority and indifference. He is a "gracious God and merciful" (Jonah 4:2). He has "no pleasure in the death of the wicked but [desires] that he may turn [repent] from his way and live" (Ezek. 33:11). His concern and love reach far beyond the people who belong to Him already. He also has "other sheep" (John 10:16) and makes His people responsible for them.

Will you help your child see God's great love in this story? And will you help him express God's love to other people?

The Editor

QUALITY RELIGIOUS BOOKS FOR CHILDREN
ARCH BOOKS
Three Men Who Walked in Fire

Three Men Who Walked in Fire

DANIEL 3 FOR CHILDREN

Written by Joann Scheck
Illustrated by Sally Mathews

Concordia Publishing House

One day in old Jerusalem
three little boys ran fast.
They hid and watched while soldiers armed
with swords and spears marched past.
"Burn down the houses! Steal the gold!"
they heard the soldiers shout.
The boys crouched very quietly,
not daring to look out.

But soon a soldier saw them there.
He quickly caught all three.

"You boys will make good slaves," he said.
"I'll take you home with me."

Though they were slaves for many years,
the boys did not despair.
"Dear God, we know You're by our side,"
they said each day in prayer.

The oldest was the smartest one—
they called him wise Shadrach.
The youngest was the strongest one—
no one could beat Meshach.
The third was liked the best of all—
no matter where he went,
Abednego brought fun and grins
and laughing merriment.

One day the king of this strange land was feeling very proud.

He thought about how great he was
until he said aloud,
"There's really nothing in the world
I cannot do or say.
Why, I could even make a god!
I'll do it right away."

"Go out," the king called to his men,
"and gather all the gold."
The soldiers quickly hurried off
to do as they were told.

One morning near the city walls
the people saw a sight
so horrible to look upon
it made them shake with fright.

An ugly statue made of gold
stood high above the town.
Its monstrous mouth was open wide,
its evil eyes glared down.

Then messengers rode everywhere
to read the king's new law.
"Hear ye! Hear ye!" they cried aloud
to everyone they saw.
"Whenever people in this land
hear music being played,
they must fall down and pray before
the god our king has made,
or else the king will have you thrown
into a fiery pen."
These words sent shivers up the spines
of even bravest men.

It wasn't long before the sound
of music filled the air,
and all the frightened people fell
upon the ground in prayer.
But suddenly the soldiers cried,
"Why can't we see Meshach?
What's happened to Abednego?
And where is wise Shadrach?"
No one could find them anywhere,
for they had stayed away;
they stayed at home and prayed to God
just as they did each day.

When he found out, the king became
as mad as he could be.
"How dare you disobey my law?"
he asked them angrily.
"Fall down upon your knees at once,
or you will soon be dead!"

But Shadrach
stepped up to the king
and slowly shook his head.
"O King," he said,
"your silly gold
is not a god at all.
It's just a hunk
of ugly junk
outside the city wall.
Our God is very powerful;
He's wise
and strong and true.
And we will pray
to Him each day
no matter what you do."

The king was furious at this—
his face turned white, then red.
"I'll show you I am stronger than
your foolish god," he said.
"Put on their coats! Now tie them up!
And make the fire burn high!"

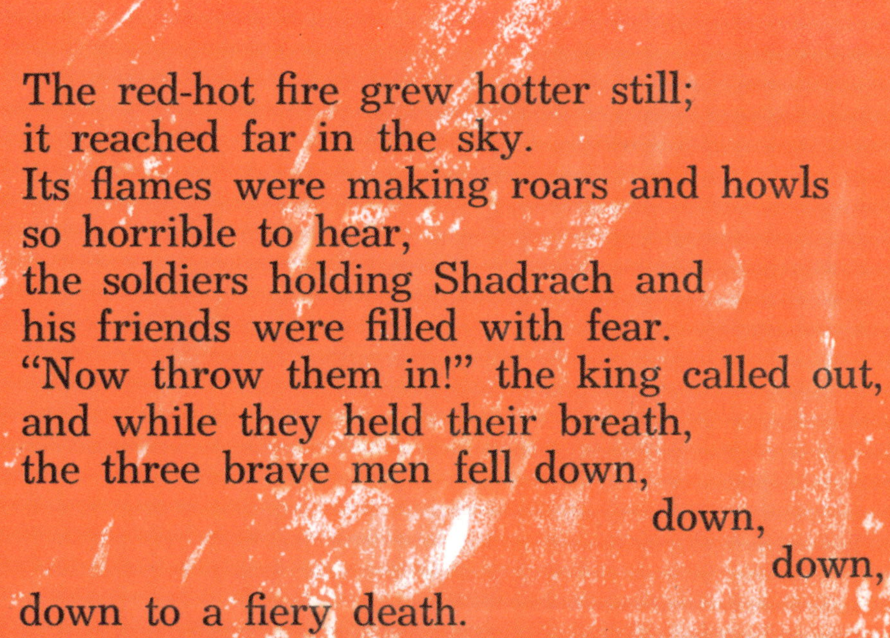

The red-hot fire grew hotter still;
it reached far in the sky.
Its flames were making roars and howls
so horrible to hear,
the soldiers holding Shadrach and
his friends were filled with fear.
"Now throw them in!" the king called out,
and while they held their breath,
the three brave men fell down,
down,
down,
down to a fiery death.

The flames rose higher now and killed
the soldiers near the pit.
The king and all the people moved
far back away from it.
The fire began to fade away,
and when the smoke had cleared,
the king could not believe his eyes
at what had now appeared.

There in the middle of the flames
four men instead of three
were walking all around the fire
alive as they could be.
The fourth man was an angel sent
by God into the pit;
he guarded so the men had not
been burned one little bit.
The king was so surprised that he
could hardly move or speak;
instead of feeling proud right now,
he felt a little weak.

At last he called, "Abednego,
Shadrach, Meshach, come out.
Why, not one hair is burned!" he said
as they turned round about.
"You truly must be men of God,
for He has set you free.
From this day on you'll be my friends
and rule along with me.
How wonderful your great God is!
Today I do command
that all my people honor Him
throughout my mighty land."

Dear Parents:

The narrative of Shadrach, Meshach, and Abednego is a story of God at work in the lives of people. God gave these three young men a strong faith. They loved and trusted God so much that they were ready to walk in fire rather than deny Him for other gods. Even the powerful king of mighty Babylon could not move them to disobey God. God was at work, keeping them in faith.

God was also at work to protect them from the flames of the fire. He sent His angel messenger to deliver them from burning to death. He used this mighty act of deliverance to lead the king and many people in the land to know Him as the true God over all the earth.

God is also at work in the lives of His people today. He shows His love and power to us in Jesus Christ. In the Gospel God shares with us the good news that Jesus delivered us from all evil by His death on the cross and His resurrection from the grave. God tells us that Jesus overcame temptations to deny His Father and to worship false gods. God sends His Spirit to lead us to faith in Him. He stands by us with His loving power when we are tempted to choose what is popular instead of what is godly, when we are urged to take the easy way instead of the right way as children of God.

Will you help your child appreciate the love of God and His deliverance in Jesus Christ? Will you strengthen your child's faith in the wonderful goodness of God, especially in time of danger and temptation?

The Editor

QUALITY RELIGIOUS BOOKS FOR CHILDREN
ARCH BOOKS
The Boy Who Gave His Lunch Away

The Boy Who Gave His Lunch Away

JOHN 6:1-15 FOR CHILDREN

Written by
Dave Hill

Illustrated by
Betty Wind

Concordia Publishing House

Joel lived a happy life
down by Lake Galilee.
"We have a farm," he liked to say,
"for Mom and Dad and me."

His dad grew barley, oats, and wheat
for baking rolls and bread.
"What we don't eat we give away,"
was what he always said.

Joel knew what Father meant,
for EVERYONE needs bread.
"But why are some folks poor," he asked,
"when we are so well fed?"

"It isn't fair at all, I know,
but someday," Father said,
"the good Messiah will be here,
and He will be our King.
Then there will be no rich or poor.
We'll all have everything!"

So Joel helped his folks at work.
He rose each day at four
and washed the pots and scrubbed the pans
and swept and mopped the floor.
He helped his dad fill up the bags
of bread to give the poor.

One warm June day a neighbor stopped to buy a loaf of bread.
"I'm on my way to see the King. He's right nearby," he said.

"A king?" said Joel.
"Right nearby?
You must be fooling me!"
The stranger shook his head.
"I'm not!
Why, people say that He
is God's Messiah – here at last!
Why don't you come and see?"

"Is this the man named Jesus, sir?"
asked Father with a smile.
"Because, if so, my son can go
and see Him for a while."

"The very man!" the neighbor cried.
"You've heard of Him, I see!"

"I've heard He's kind and loves the Lord.
That's good enough for me!"

"You'd better take this lunch along, my boy," his mother said. "I've packed you up two fish and five small loaves of barley bread."

"I won't need that!" cried Joel. "Why, the King will feed the poor!"

But Father told him, "Take it, son," as they went out the door.

So up the road, with lunch in hand,
the two went with a smile.
They soon came to a noisy crowd
stretched out for half a mile.
"He must be near! We'll see the King
in just a little while!"

"That's Jesus there!"
a voice called out,
and Joel turned to see.
There stood a man
as plain and poor
as any man could be!

He ran up close
where he could see,
and hear what Jesus said.
"Is this the King –
this plain, poor man?
I'm glad I brought
some bread!"

Then Jesus spoke; His voice was strong:
"Bring all the sick to Me!"
And Joel stared as lame folks walked
and blind men cried: "I see!"

As Joel watched, he saw the sick
made whole and well and strong.
"Our King! Our King!" a shout rose up
from all who came along.

Then Jesus turned
and raised a hand
and spoke out
loud and clear:
"The kingdom that
God promised you
you see
already here!

"The kingdom
the Messiah brings
is full of
love and joy.
It's like a happy
dinner that
a king gives
for his boy."

The day grew short, and someone cried:
"I wish we had some bread!"
A man beside the Teacher spoke:
"How will these folks be fed?"

When Joel heard, he ran right up:
"I have some bread and fish.
I'll gladly share them with the crowd
if that is what you wish!"

"Five loaves? Two fish? For all this mob?"
asked one man with a frown.
But Jesus took the food and said,
"Have everyone sit down."

"We thank You, Father," Jesus prayed
and blessed and broke the bread.
Then His disciples passed it out
till ALL THE CROWD was fed.

"A miracle!" somebody cried.
"There's food for all to share!"
The helpers even gathered up
twelve baskets full to spare.

“Hooray! Hooray!” the people cheered.
“Shall we crown Jesus king?
He’ll always give us what we need,
and we’ll have everything!”
But Jesus turned and hurried off.
He wanted no such thing!

DEAR PARENTS:

Like Joel, people in New Testament times looked for the promised Messiah to come and establish His kingdom. In their deep longing they hoped for a time when the hungry would have enough to eat and the poor would have all their needs supplied.

In Jesus, the Messiah, the kingdom of God came according to promise. Jesus announced the Kingdom in words: "The time is fulfilled, and the kingdom of God is at hand" (Mark 1:15). He performed many signs to indicate the coming of God's kingdom, or gracious rule, over men. The feeding of the 5,000 with five loaves and two fishes is such a sign. This feeding miracle reminds us of parables in which Jesus compared the kingdom of God to a great dinner banquet. He invites all people, good and bad, rich and poor. God provides for the needs of people in generous abundance at this banquet. There is plenty for all, even when our faith is too small to see how God can provide. Resources at the banquet may be limited, but Christ uses them to feed the thousands who come to Him.

The people who were fed by the loaves and fishes were impressed by Jesus' powers. They wanted to make Him a bread king to satisfy their hunger and other needs of daily life. Because they misunderstood the King and His kingdom, "Jesus withdrew again to the hills by Himself" (John 6:15). He is more than a supplier of free bread. He is the "Bread of Life" (John 6:35), who brings the rule of God to us and gives us His goodness and love.

Will you help your child see the meaning of our story as the work of Christ putting God's kingdom into action? Will you help him experience the joy and abundance of life in Christ's church?

THE EDITOR

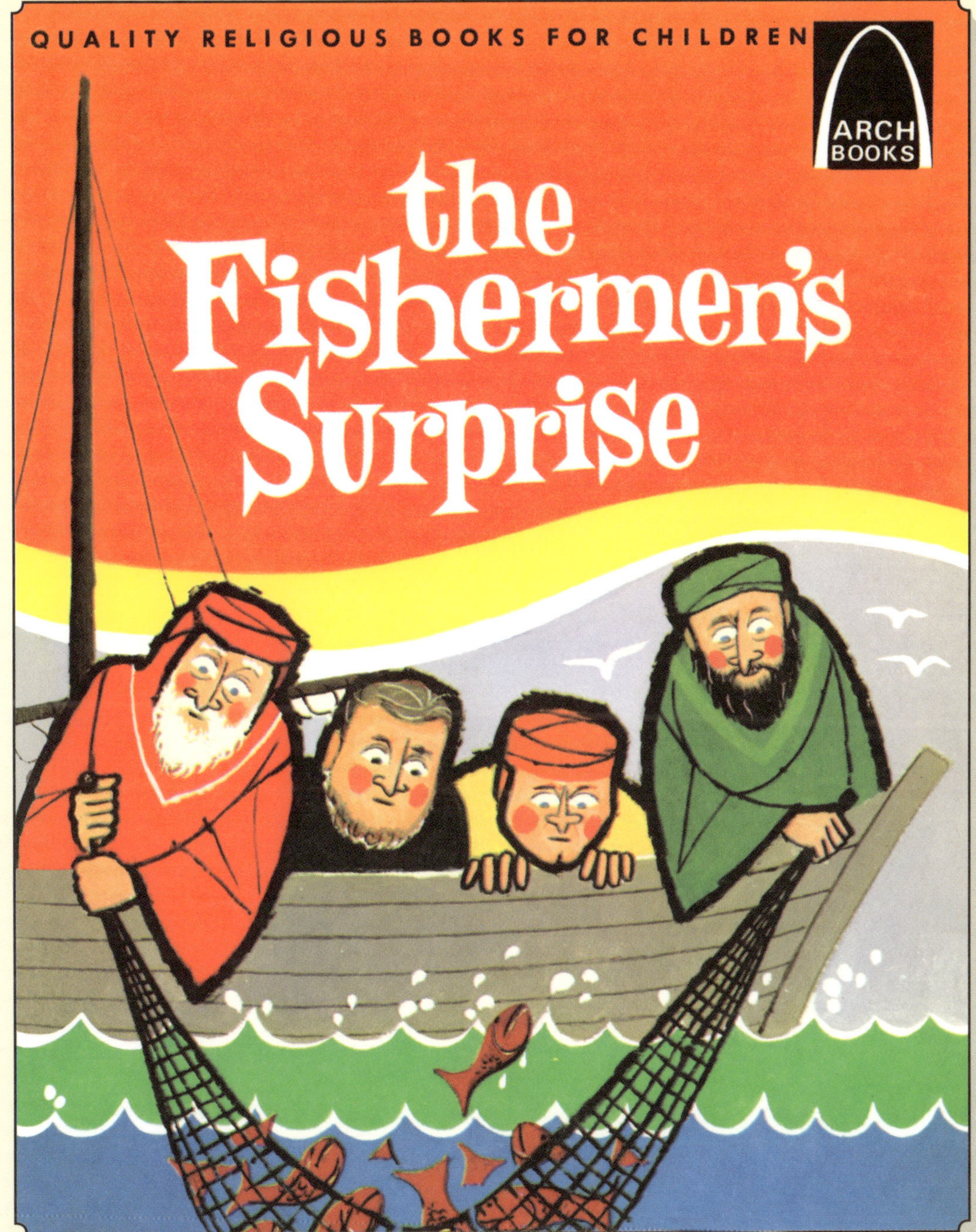
QUALITY RELIGIOUS BOOKS FOR CHILDREN
ARCH BOOKS
the Fishermen's Surprise

LUKE 5:1-11 AND JOHN 21 FOR CHILDREN

Written by Alyce Bergey

Illustrated by Bill Behm

Concordia Publishing House

As Jesus walked one morning by
the Sea of Galilee,
He saw some fishermen at work.
Said Jesus, "Follow Me!
I'll teach you how to help Me in
the work that I will do."
"Yes, Master," called the fishermen.
"We'll come and follow You."

The men all left their boats and nets.
They went with Christ instead.
"From now on you'll be catching men,
not fish," the Master said.

Then, helping Jesus teach and heal,
from place to place they trod,
not bringing fish in from the sea
but bringing men to God.

When Jesus died His friends were sad.
Alone, they wept and said,
"The One who was our Master and
our dearest Friend is dead."

One day went by. Two days went by.
The third day dawned, and then—
at evening Jesus came to them.
He was alive again!

“Don’t be afraid,” His puzzled friends
all heard their Master say.
“I had to die and rise again
to take men’s sins away.”
The men rejoiced; this truly was
the Master, they could see!
He told them, “I will meet you soon.
Go back to Galilee.”

The men walked back to Galilee.
They waited there, and then
one afternoon they went and sat
down by the sea again.
They watched the fishing boats go out.
The setting sun was red.
"I miss the Master. Oh, I wish
that He were here!" John said.

"Yes, many days have passed since we
have seen Him," Thomas cried.
The men all sadly shook their heads.
"What shall we do?" James sighed.

"Let's fish!" said Peter.
"Yes, let's fish!"
the other men said too.
They found their nets and oars. And then,
just like they used to do,

they climbed into their boat, and as
the sun sank low and set,
they rowed out on the water and
let down their fishing net.
The stars soon twinkled up above.
The yellow moon was bright.
The men let down their fishing net
time after time that night.

Each time they pulled it in, they looked
for fish, but there were none!
Yes, though they fished all night, they caught
no fish — not even ONE!
"Have we forgotten how to fish?"
asked Andrew, looking glum.
"Yes," Peter said, "our luck is bad.
I wish we hadn't come!"

The sun was rising. From the shore
the men heard someone call,
"Do you have any fish there, lads?"
They cried, "No, none at all!"
"Then let your net down on the right,"
He called back from the shore.

Surprised, the men let down their net
into the sea once more.
They waited; then they grabbed the ropes
and all began to pull.
Then —

"FISH!" cried Peter.
"FISH!" cried John.
"Oh, look! Our net is full!"

The men could not believe their eyes.
"We caught no fish all night.
Now look at all these big, big fish!"
they shouted in delight.
"It must be Jesus on the shore!"
John said to Peter then.
Yes, Peter thought, it's Jesus, come
to help us once again.

He jumped into the sea and swam toward shore, where Jesus stood. The rest came in the little boat as quickly as they could.

“Oh, Jesus, Jesus!” cried the men when they had reached the shore. “How glad we are to see You! Please don't leave us anymore!”

Just then they saw a fire of coals
with cooking fish and bread.
"Now bring some fish that you have caught.
We need more," Jesus said.
"You made our breakfast, Master!" His
surprised and pleased friends cried.
"You worked all night. I knew you would
be hungry," He replied.

Big Peter ran and pulled their catch
of fish in from the sea.
And on the shore they counted them—
one hundred fifty-three!
Then Jesus put some on the fire.
When they had cooked awhile,
"Come now and have your breakfast, lads!"
He called out with a smile.

The Master's friends sat round the fire.
He gave them fish and bread.
Now Jesus said to Peter and
the rest, when they were fed,
"Feed all My sheep and lambs!" And then
He gave them this command:

"Tell all the world that I have come.
Go into every land.
Tell red and yellow, black and white
until all people know.
I shall be with you every day
and everywhere you go!"

Dear Parents:

The actions of Jesus as the Servant of God and the Redeemer of the world came as an unexpected surprise to the people of His time. Not the least surprised were some fishermen at the Sea of Galilee. They were surprised at the great number of fish they caught after His command: "Put out into the deep, and let down your nets for a catch." (Luke 5:4)

They were surprised at His words: "Do not be afraid; henceforth you will be catching men" (Luke 5:10). As His disciples, these fishermen were surprised at the many signs and acts of mercy Jesus performed. They were surprised by the events of His trial and crucifixion. The sudden appearance of the risen Christ behind locked doors on Easter evening and His words: "As the Father has sent Me, even so I send you," came as a great surprise.

The surprise in John 21 comes on another fishing trip. After catching nothing all night, they follow the advice of a stranger on shore and catch a netful. A breakfast of fish and bread awaits them. The stranger is their risen Lord. He strengthens these simple fishermen as His disciples to bring the Gospel to the world, to feed His lambs and to tend His sheep.

Will you help your child appreciate the surprising acts of Jesus in His love for us? Will you show your child the surprise of God's loving presence — at a beach breakfast for tired fishermen or at a picnic of happy children? And can you express the surprising joy that you and your child are among those sent to share the love of Christ with all people?

The Editor

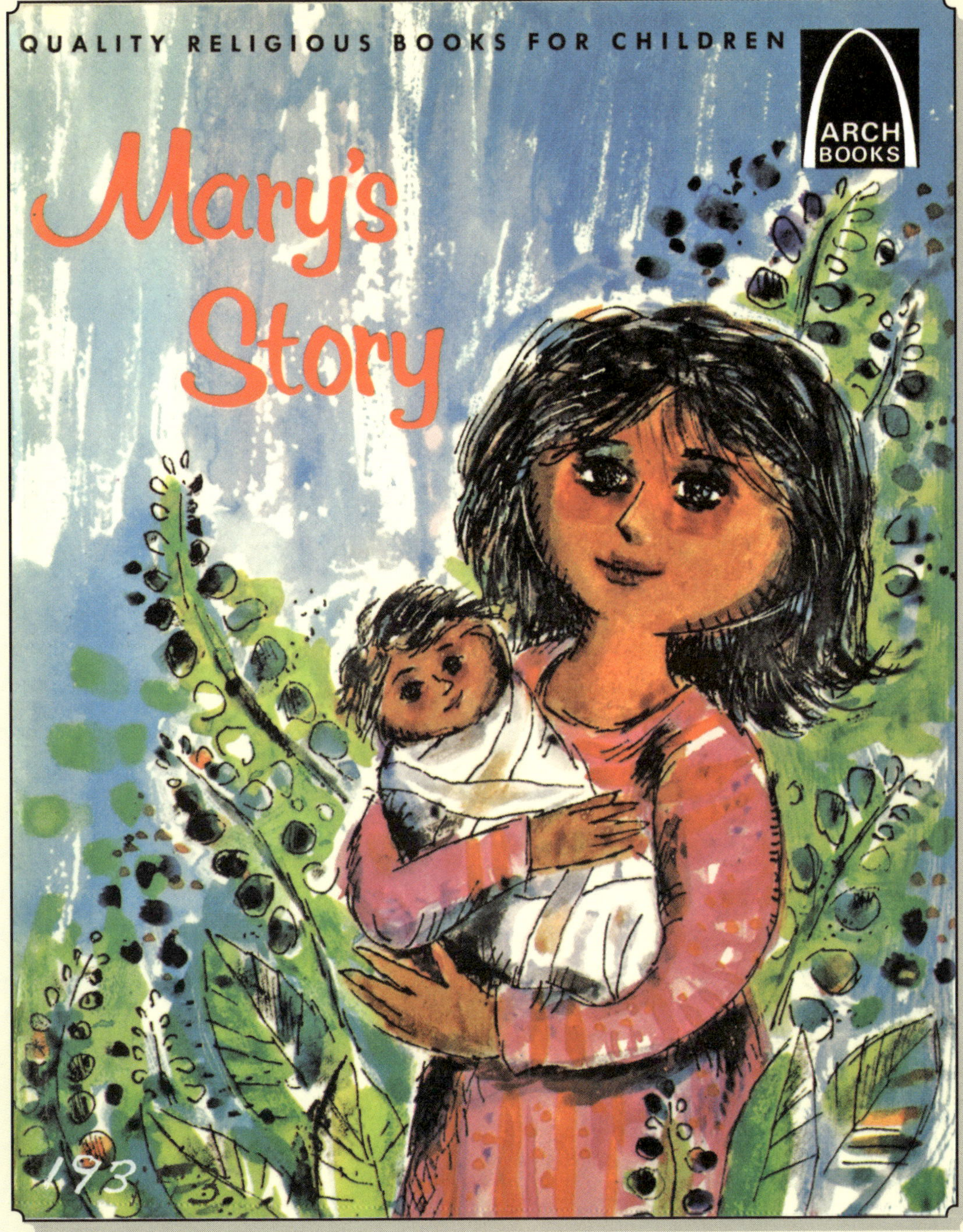
QUALITY RELIGIOUS BOOKS FOR CHILDREN
ARCH BOOKS
Mary's Story
193

Mary's Story

LUKE 1:5 – 2:18 FOR CHILDREN

Written by M. M. Brem
Illustrated by Sally Mathews

Concordia Publishing House

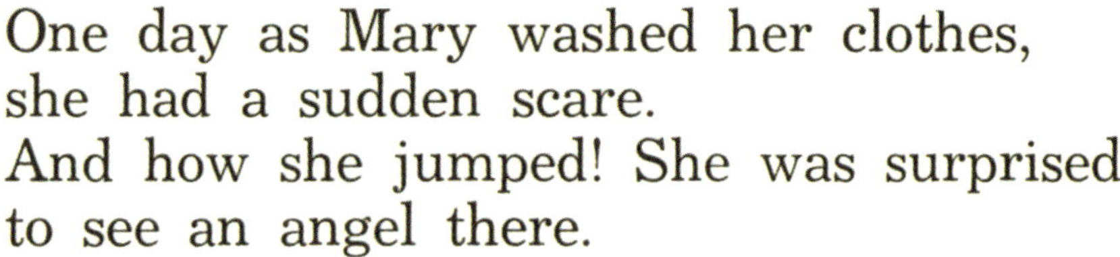

One day as Mary washed her clothes,
she had a sudden scare.
And how she jumped! She was surprised
to see an angel there.

Before she had a chance to speak,
the angel said, "Don't fear.
I have important news for you.
Our God has sent me here.

"For you will have a baby soon,
and He will be God's Son.
His name is Jesus. He will come
in love for everyone."

"But I'm not married yet," she said.
"So how can this be true?"
"That isn't hard for God," he said.
"There's nothing He can't do.

"He'll send the Holy Spirit down.
But that's not all God's done.
For though Elizabeth is old,
she, too, will have a son."

And Mary said, "It's wonderful
that I may serve the Lord.
Whatever God wants, I will do
according to His Word."

And when the angel disappeared,
then Mary packed to go.
"The angel told me what to do.
I know where I will go.

"I'll go and see Elizabeth;
it's just the thing to do.
And I would like to know if she
has seen the angel too."

She said, "Good-by," and hurried off.
It was not long before
Elizabeth heard Mary knock.
She hurried to the door.

Elizabeth saw Mary there.
Her heart was filled with joy.
"Great wonders have been done," she said,
"I, too, will have a boy!

"Our God has blessed us both," she said,
"but you're the honored one.
You are the one God chose to be
the mother of His Son."

And Mary sang a song of praise.
"Lord, I believe that You
will send Your Son to save us as
You promised You would do."

That night they sat and talked when there
was nothing else to do.
And Mary said, "I wondered if you saw the angel too."

Elizabeth said, "No, not I!
He did not come to me!
But Zechariah was the one
the angel came to see.

"An angel suddenly appeared
quite close to where he stood,
and Zechariah shook with fear
as anybody would.

"The angel said, 'Don't be afraid.
I have good news for you.
You know that you are very old
and that your wife is too.

" 'But God has a surprise for you,
a very special one.
Our God decided it is time
to give you both a son.

“ ‘You’ll call him John. He will prepare
the people for God’s Son.
He’ll baptize men and preach *good news*
and say, “God’s Son is come!” ’

“My husband said, ‘How will I know
the things you say are true?’
The sign the angel gave is why
he cannot talk to you.”

And Mary stayed with them three months.

But then she said one day,
"It's time for me to go back home.

I should be on my way."

She said, “Good-by,” and hurried home.
When Joseph married her,
he said, “Now we must make our home,
so where would you prefer?”

“Let’s stay right here,” she said. But God
had other plans for them,
and so He had them leave their home
and go to Bethlehem.

The town was crowded,
rooms were scarce
when they arrived that day.

A stable was the only place
where both of them could stay.

And late that night God's Son was born,
and Jesus was His name.
But everyone in town slept on
and didn't know He came.

Some shepherds were the first to know.
While tending sheep that night,
an angel suddenly they saw.
The hills were bright with light.

“Don’t be afraid,” the angel said.
“Just go to Bethlehem,
and you will find your Savior there.
Now go and worship Him.”

"He's come!" one said. "The Savior whom
we've waited for is here!"
"Let's go and see!" another said.
"That town is very near."

More angels came to them before
they went to Bethlehem.
"Glory be to God on high!"
the angels sang to them.

"Peace on earth! Goodwill to men!
God's Son has come to earth!"
After that they went and found
the place of Jesus' birth.

They found the stable where He was
and quietly went in
to worship Jesus, who had come
to save us from our sin.

DEAR PARENTS:

The birth of Jesus is the central point of the familiar Christmas Gospel, but St. Luke tells us that some wonderful things happened before He was born in the stable in Bethlehem.

The angel messenger paid a surprise visit to the maiden Mary and announced that she would bear the promised Son. When she questioned how this could be, the angel gave the answer: The Holy Spirit would come and make it possible for her to conceive, for God can do anything. In childlike faith young Mary accepted the Word of the Lord and promised to be His servant.

Bursting to share the news, she hurried to visit her cousin Elizabeth. Can you imagine their excitement as they discussed the wonders of God? Elizabeth would become the mother of John the Baptist, and Mary would give birth to the promised Savior.

Will you help your child see the wonder of God's grace in choosing a humble maid to be the mother of Jesus? Will you lead him to see the joy of Mary in believing the Word of God and in doing what He asked? Above all, will you share the Good News that Jesus Christ is born to take away evil and to make us happy children of God?

THE EDITOR

The Arch® Book Bible Story Library

Bible Beginnings

59-1577 The Fall into Sin
59-1534 The First Brothers
59-2206 A Man Named Noah
59-1511 Noah's 2-by-2 Adventure
59-1560 The Story of Creation
59-2239 Where Did the World Come From?

The Old Testament

59-1502 Abraham's Big Test
59-2244 Abraham, Sarah, and Isaac
59-2229 Daniel and the Lions
59-1559 David and Goliath
59-1593 David and His Friend Jonathan
59-2220 Deborah Saves the Day
59-1543 Elijah Helps the Widow
59-2251 Ezekiel and the Dry Bones
59-1567 The Fiery Furnace
59-1570 God Calls Abraham . . . God Calls You!
59-1587 God Provides Victory through Gideon
59-2279 God Saves Jerusalem
59-1523 God's Fire for Elijah
59-1542 Good News for Naaman
59-2223 How Enemies Became Friends
59-2247 Isaac Blesses Jacob and Esau
59-1538 Jacob's Dream
59-1539 Jericho's Tumbling Walls
59-2246 Jonah, the Runaway Prophet
59-1514 Jonah and the Very Big Fish
59-2233 Joseph, Jacob's Favorite Son
59-2216 King Josiah and God's Book
59-1583 The Lord Calls Samuel
59-2219 Moses and the Bronze Snake
59-1607 Moses and the Long Walk
59-2266 The Mystery of the Moving Hand
59-1535 A Mother Who Prayed
59-2249 One Boy, One Stone, One God
59-2253 Queen Esther Visits the King
59-2211 Ruth and Naomi
59-2276 Samson
59-1586 The Ten Commandments
59-1608 The Ten Plagues
59-2263 The Tower of Babel
59-1550 Tiny Baby Moses
59-1530 Tried and True Job
59-2260 The 23rd Psalm
59-1603 Zerubbabel Rebuilds the Temple

The New Testament

59-1580 The Coming of the Holy Spirit
59-2259 The Great Commission
59-2207 His Name Is John
59-1532 Jailhouse Rock
59-1520 Jesus and the Family Trip
59-2277 Jesus and the Rich Young Man
59-1588 Jesus Calls His Disciples
59-2215 Jesus Shows His Glory
59-2270 Lydia Believes
59-1521 Mary and Martha's Dinner Guest
59-2269 Nicodemus and Jesus
59-2227 Paul's Great Basket Caper
59-2267 The Pentecost Story
59-1578 Philip and the Ethiopian
59-1601 Saul's Conversion
59-1574 Timothy Joins Paul
59-2222 Twelve Ordinary Men
59-1599 Zacchaeus

Arch® Book Companions

59-2232 The Fruit of the Spirit
59-1609 God, I've Gotta Talk to You
59-1575 The Lord's Prayer
59-1562 My Happy Birthday Book
59-2271 Best-Loved Christmas Stories
59-2272 Best-Loved Parables of Jesus
59-2273 Best-Loved Miracles of Jesus
59-2274 Best-Loved Easter Stories

Christmas Arch® Books

59-1579 Baby Jesus Is Born
59-1544 Baby Jesus Visits the Temple
59-1553 Born on Christmas Morn
59-2261 The Christmas Angels
59-1605 The Christmas Message
59-2225 The Christmas Promise
59-1546 Joseph's Christmas Story
59-1499 Mary's Christmas Story
59-1584 My Merry Christmas Arch® Book
59-2278 O Bethlehem
59-2252 Oh, Holy Night!
59-1537 On a Silent Night
59-2243 Once Upon a Clear Dark Night
59-2234 The Shepherds Shook in Their Shoes
59-2268 The Songs of Christmas
59-1594 Star of Wonder
59-2209 When Jesus Was Born

Easter Arch® Books

59-1551 Barabbas Goes Free
59-2205 The Centurion at the Cross
59-1516 The Day Jesus Died
59-2213 The Easter Gift
59-2221 The Easter Stranger
59-2275 The Easter Surprise
59-1602 The Easter Victory
59-2265 From Adam to Easter
59-1582 Good Friday
59-1585 Jesus Enters Jerusalem
59-1561 Jesus Returns to Heaven
59-2248 John's Easter Story
59-1592 Mary Magdalene's Easter Story
59-1564 My Happy Easter Arch® Book
59-2258 The Gardens of Easter
59-2231 The Resurrection
59-1517 The Story of the Empty Tomb
59-1504 Thomas, the Doubting Disciple
59-1501 The Very First Lord's Supper
59-1541 The Week That Led to Easter

Parables and Lessons of Jesus

59-2257 Jesus and the Canaanite Woman
59-1589 Jesus and the Woman at the Well
59-1500 Jesus Blesses the Children
59-1595 Jesus, My Good Shepherd
59-2245 Jesus Teaches Us Not to Worry
59-1540 Jesus Washes Peter's Feet
59-2264 The Lesson of the Tree and Its Fruit
59-1606 The Lost Coin
59-2235 The Parable of the Ten Bridesmaids
59-2218 The Parable of the Lost Sheep
59-2224 The Parable of the Prodigal Son
59-2262 The Parable of the Seeds
59-2210 The Parable of the Talents
59-2254 The Parable of the Woman and the Judge
59-2250 The Parable of the Workers in the Vineyard
59-1512 The Seeds That Grew and Grew
59-1503 The Story of Jesus' Baptism and Temptation
59-1596 The Story of the Good Samaritan
59-2214 The Widow's Offering
59-2208 The Wise and Foolish Builders

Miracles Jesus Performed

59-1531 Down through the Roof
59-1568 Get Up, Lazarus!
59-1604 The Great Catch of Fish
59-1581 Jesus Calms the Storm
59-1598 Jesus' First Miracle
59-2230 Jesus Heals Blind Bartimaeus
59-2255 Jesus Heals the Man at the Pool
59-2236 Jesus Heals the Centurion's Servant
59-2226 Jesus Wakes the Little Girl
59-1597 Jesus Walks on the Water
59-1558 A Meal for Many
59-2212 The Thankful Leper
59-2280 The Wedding at Cana
59-1510 What's for Lunch?